the womxn

poems by

jamilla vandyke-bailey

Finishing Line Press
Georgetown, Kentucky

the womxn

Copyright © 2023 by jamilla vandyke-bailey
ISBN 979-8-88838-409-1 First Edition
All rights reserved under International and Pan-American Copyright Conventions. No part of this book may be reproduced in any manner whatsoever without written permission from the publisher, except in the case of brief quotations embodied in critical articles and reviews.

ACKNOWLEDGMENTS

ubuntu: karyn vandyke, kathryne vandyke, kathryn white, kimberly vandyke, karla vandyke, traci vandyke, chevanese vandyke, germaine ross, bailey chandler, brenda chaney, christina chaney, mikka mcqueen, tiana mcqueen, keisha bailey, shawnda chaney, iesha gizaw, sharon depina, barbara rose, dorothy rose, lita bailey, stacey cannady, grizelda cannady, betty walker. and of course, thank you to my father: dana bailey who was determined to raise a strong black woman—because he *did that*. and thank you to my son, dana-morrison sellassie awuye who has made me a better woman.

thank you to those who inspired me and those who allowed me to use their stories as inspiration: alexa jones, alice walker, anne sexton, ashley cullinane, audre lorde, bhanu kapil, bianca bailey, chevanese vandyke, dayjuana day, jacqueline woodson, kate zulaski, keiylah rivers, leah rose-walker, lupita aquino, madeleine brunson, marisha averya, maya angelou, mckenzie hurder, meaghan rateau, myriam gurba serrano, nicole b, ocatvia butler, rebecca jeannick ndwana, sandra cisneros, shacoya lothery, siarra freeman, sylvia plath, tanicia pratt, toni morrison, tonya ingram, victoria wagner.

Publisher: Leah Huete de Maines
Editor: Christen Kincaid
Cover Art: Evie Shaffer
Author Photo: Jaclyn Poeschl
Cover Design: jamilla vandyke-bailey

Order online: www.finishinglinepress.com
also available on amazon.com

Author inquiries and mail orders:
Finishing Line Press
P. O. Box 1626
Georgetown, Kentucky 40324
U. S. A.

table of contents

i. how was "girl," first defined for you
    girl one 1
    1. wash and put dry 2
    girl two 3
    girl three... 4
    i found myself not boy 5
    close your legs 6
    did you know.. 7

ii. who stole your body from you and how did you get it back?
    who stole your body.. 11
    ways to heal #17 12
    i was emancipated 13
    the body was loaned... 14
    sovereignty... 15
    y'know.. 16
    after the baby.. 17
    a gospel as told by womxn.. 18
    i forgot to realize 19
    i was six.. 20
    "nobody…" 21
    being fat 22

iii. what is the hardest lesson loving your mother has taught you?
    ways to heal #22 25
    i inherited mommas fields... 26
    dear momma,.. 27
    some mommas.. 28
    my grandmother died an islander 29
    a baby is crying 30
    ma,.. 31

iv. what do you know about cleaning up blood?
    1. try 35
    and another gospel as told by womxn 36
    1. remember 37
    blood on cotton panty fabric..38

v. how can we love you better? and you, us?
    love me better..41
    ways to heal #1 42
    i need you 43
    look at me 44
    sis, come sit with me 45

for: dana-morrison sellassie awuye
of womxn born; of womxn raised

for: the womxn in the words
of womxn raised, of womxn born

i. how was "girl," first defined for you?

girl one

girl (gər(-ə)l), n. [pl. girls (gər(-ə)l'z)],
a female child from birth to adulthood;
    synonym: pink; daughter;
    synonym: pink; a young womxn;
    synonym: pink; pink; pink

sometimes offensive: a single or married womxn of any age.
antonym: pink pink pink; gentle; graceful; warm; a sweetheart;

often offensive: a female servant or employee.
    synonym: pink; gentle; graceful; warm
    antonym: warm; graceful; gentle; pink pink pink

informal: a female friend;
used as a friendly way of addressing a womxn or girl.
synonym: gentle
    synonym: warm
    synonym: graceful
    synonym: pink
    synonym: you
    ~~**synonym**: vagina~~

1. wash and put dry

1. wash and put dry
2. don't cook sweet oil
3. soak after you take a wash
      soak overnight before you cook
4. sing
5. eat your food like you are becoming
4. sing
6. speak
2. don't eat street flies
4. sing all and never
7. sew; sew
8. hem yourself to look becoming
9. iron; iron
10. grow far from the house
       grow plenty of water
11. sweep a corner
       sweep a whole house
       sweep a yard
12. smile too much
       smile completely
13. set a table
       set a table for dinner
       set a table for lunch
       set a table for breakfast
14. behave in the presence of men
1. wash your own spit
2. don't play marbles
15. pick flowers
2. don't throw blackbirds
16. make bread, pepper, pot, good medicine
17. throw away a child before it falls on you
18. bully a man, love a man
19. feel bad about giving it
20. move on
16. make ends meet
       make it fresh
21. be the kind of womxn let near the bread

After "Girl" by Jamaica Kincaid (1978)

girl two

girl: an act of separation, a partition, a metaphysical isolation
see: "that's girl stuff"
    example: dolls, pink, dolls that are pink, and pink dolls.

    example: grace, warmth, graceful warmth, a warming grace.

    example: gentle, you, you being gentle, being gentle with you

see also: shed it like a ureteral lining after your breasts come in
    example: genderless, gender neutral, pinkless, pinkful

girl three

girl:
syn: sunday school teacher, a layer of words
      or: loving female, caring female, cooking female

syn: church water for others, a nailing thirst for self
      or: loving, caring, and cooking softly and compassionately

syn: not rough, not rough or loud, not rough or loud or tough

syn: performing under lights, under eyes, under lightning eyes

syn: washing hands clean, cleaning hands, washing clean hands
      or: washing with love or care, carefully washing love and cooking

syn: an order: do or don't do, don't do, do or don't, do or do, or don't

syn: a concept: like school, like water, like not rough, like under eyes

syn: a kind: like hands, like washing, like atlas derived, like doing

i found myself not boy

i found myself not boy, but defined boy, and given boy.

boy standards and boy expectations came with corrections
because i was not boy, but acting boy, and acting boy badly.

soon, a boy who is not a boy becomes a man who is not a man;
given man standards and man expectations with corrections.

all without my consent, all without my permission, all without me.

i was casted as boy, and forced to perform for everyone
and i performed the fuck out of that role because
it was all i had, it was all i was given, and it was all i was to be.

but one midnight, i found myself and returned everything else.
i gave myself permission to become my own definition: womxn.

close your legs

close your legs when you're sitting
cross them at the ankle not the knee

dress in dresses dressed in trimmings and lace
not that kind of lace. the christian kind.

pink. or purple. or yellowy clear.

     daddy wanted a boy
     gave me biker jackets
     gave me matching tims
     gave me durango boots
     gave me straightbacks

but then at puberty i found in the attic,
vanity mirrors and vanity affairs.
and spoke myself into girl

     mirror
     mirror

i am girl.
i am pretty.
i am pretty girl.
i am girl girl girl girl.
i am pretty pretty pretty pretty.

i close my legs at the ankles
in lace trimmed dresses called spring.

did you know

Did you know that girl is a
d e r o g a t o r y term
it makes you unidentifiable
colors you incapable,
left without value.

the men in my family called me girl
and so did the world
and so did we

and so we were.

ii. who stole your body from you and how did you get it back?

who stole your body

who stole your body from you?

>he did but we were Y O U N G. you know?
>it was kid shit. unguided and abandoned.
>he stole it from me, but we were Y O U N G.

how did you get it back?

>i was venerable

Venerable. Adjective. Given a great deal of respect.

i think you mean vulnerable?

>i was vulnerable.
>vulnerable and forgiving of him.
>venerable and accepting of me.

~~and is it e~~

>i'm getting there. you know?
>i was so Y O U N G and we both were.
>and i don't want to abandon myself.
>i don't wanna live it stolen and unguided.
>i want a future too. i want to forgive myself too.
>so i take it day by day by day by day.

>i mean i was five
>and he was my brother's cousin
>i am never not five
>i am always five
>five forever
>forever and ever and ever five
>and i am five day by day by day by day.

ways to heal (#17)

ways to heal (#17)

pray until you are empty, and even then—still.

go to god
        not the one that was discovered for you,
        but the one that you forged yourself.

ask god
        to introduce you to yourself,
        suitcases, and scars, and singed sinew.

go to yourself
        both exposed without explanation
        and mutter words of love that you do not mean
        because you do not mean it, *yet*.

ask yourself
        to be kind, to be a prayer, to be in prayer
        and in kindness, enfold yourself inside out.

pray until you are worthy, and even then—still.

i was emancipated

i was emancipated a decade ago
free from all this damp blackness
spreading through my cartilage like a fog.

liberated from the bruising pressure
of choosing to loan you a piece of my love.

i should have caught it earlier.

should have heard the ache in my spine,
a sign that i was nursing a sickness inside.

how long have i begun to avoid the
strangeness of my laugh without laughter?
when did flinching with apologies
mark my mouth like a molding native tongue?

i thought i was better than that.

but you drew me sopping wet with lies:
confused, conflicted, contradicting
the person i had built myself up to be.

~~you made me~~
~~i let you~~
~~we~~

i have learned to let go of the chafing possibilities
of past tense verbs that could never take hold.

i have heard of the gospel where there is only reality.
there be only two things: what you did and what i did.
my own accountability without the stench of shame.

a decade free is not without pains and prayers
but it is without you, and within the me i need.

the body was loaned

the body was loaned to the mother
to carry the child who was also on loan.

the father with the shadow of a manchild
couldn't stomach his own spinelessness;
not when we was making a solstice in our navel.

and so he taught himself how to dismantle us.

what was once teasing soured into sandpaper.

he forgot the words beautiful, and pregnant; so
he called us a housefly, a flea, and a bedbug.
a strip tease, a whore house, and a hypocrite.

these words, every day these words settled
into his understanding of the one he made mother.

and that is why, he said, that is why he had to
use his hands to reorganize our orbital bone,
the enamel of our teeth and our tin tongue.

he became blind with the residue of insecurity
and he tried to break us. to break our body.

the body that was loaned to the mother
so we could carry the child who was also on loan.

and every time he couldn't break us.

and he would try again, and again, and again.

until we made ourselves into a trapdoor
and hid the child and the mother
who was also on loan.

sovereignty

sovereignty (noun)

a: supreme power of authority
think: jurisdiction
    —but not: law; not civil
think: dominion
    —but not: bible; not gen 1:26-28
    —more like: good touch, bad tough
    —more like: good fuck, bad fuck
    —better yet, like: "no" without teeth

b: the authority to govern itself
think: independence
think: self-government, or self-rule
    —like:

y'know

                                                y'know
one thing i always prided myself on is
no one stole my body from me.
no one took it.
i didn't misplace it.

well,
then.
what happened to you?

                        i gave it to them
—proudly and with teeth—
not a lease
not a rental
not a loan.
borrow me,
i said preemptively.

well,
then.
what happened to you?

                                      i said,
borrow me
preemptively.
it was my choice.
i was in control.
I SAID, *BORROW ME.*

well,
then.
what happened to—

                 and even when it hurt
i was so proud of me.
proud that i gave it to them
free of charge,
not a lease
not a rental
not a loan,
fuck it, not even borrowed,
just free of charge

after the baby

after the baby
my body turned childhood home
full of empty furniture still warm with life.

the windows were gauzy with use and history
and there was only wallpaper in the kitchen corners.

i have to make clean of the dust with my own fingertips,
add some lights taken from a smile i had hidden away.

and then i will lay beside my own self
on the living room floor and laugh
and fill up every creak in this house with ourselves
and the doors and mirrors will ring with us;
welcoming us home.

a gospel as told by womxn

    many people stole my body
    my mother and our inability to accept
    that cousin that touched
    that older boy that touched
    all of the
        two-stepping and spinning
        kissing closely and roughly
        being a girl-kid in love
        being a girl-adult in love
        dressing like im in love with me

    it's a theft always needing
        to act, to please, to be pleased, and be.

    stealing isn't just taking,
        it's a force
        it's confinement
        it's punishment
        it's absent of consent
        it's everything outside of this

i forgot to realize

i forgot to realize that i am growing in to myself

toenails rotting backwards into full river beds;
hair splitting into loud waves of a wet depth;
bones aching with ash;
      with weight;
      with dreams dead from weight;
           from the weight of waiting
                for this life to taste less like contempt.

less like clocking in clocking out clocking in late
like robbing peter to pay paul and still coming up short
like clocking out and clocking in and never clocking out

when did i sew myself into this ritual?

was it handed down like myrtle trees and infancy?
      my daughter's momma
      my momma, our momma
      her momma's momma's momma's momma
          momma gotta work, baby

momma working and begging god for another day
spend working and polishing the pasture with her sweat
heavy with the sweet weight of always waiting. wading.

i am tired for them and for my damn self but i can't stop
and if i don't then who will and i got kids to pay
and bills to feed and this stale pride picking me clean
and maybe some day i-
i   i   i   i   i   i   i

i forgot to realize that i am growing in to myself

i was six

i was six but my mom worked nights
the babysitter was a mother too
        three kids: boy twin, girl twin, and small boy

the boy twin was all adjectives and descriptors
        all synonyms for domineering
        and synonyms for careful

the boy twin made things
        made fun of us
        made into our space
        made us do things
                made me kiss the small boy
                made me waste my first kiss

the boy twin was all verbs and actions
        pushing
        poking
        smacking
        bullying
        making making making making
        and unmaking

"nobody"

nobody and it wasn't but
by the grace of god

being fat

being fat and kinned

being fat and little girl
        fat and little girl and near men
        and near men who are older
        who are older and see me
                and see me and touch me

being fat and little girl
        fat and little girl liking boys
        liking boys who like fat girls
        who like fat girls who are quiet
        are quiet and fat and keep secrets
                secrets like dating; like loving

being fat and womxn
        fat and womxn wanting men
        wanting men who like fat womxn
        fat womxn who have fat like me
                fat that don't sit right on bones
                fat that's plus plus plus plus size
                fat not thick not bbl not body made

being fat and kinned and little girl and womxn and alive
and alive as a fat womxn in the world
in a world that wants me little and girly and skinny
and to kin that wants me little and girly and skinny and alive
and alive and alive and alive and alive and not fat and not me

iii. what is the hardest lesson loving your mother has taught you?

ways to heal (#22)

1. it will be a struggle, so spend a month of sundays
teaching your arms a new translation for "struggle."

say, "struggle"

and make it a noun
        synonymous with: your temporary homestead
        synonymous with: a murky asylum of growth

say, "struggle"

and make it a verb
        1. to shed toxins from yourself, painfully and dutifully
        2. to sift through mud in search of the gold you hid there

say, "struggle"

and make it an adjective
        copy and paste definitions for "necessary," and "pre-ordained"

cloak your wrists and elbows and thorough shoulders
in this new dance of struggle. as a noun, as a verb, as an adjective.

practice how to carry the struggle and make it part of you.
not like a shirt but like a rawhide that holds tight like god's armor.

i inherited momma's fields

i inherited momma's fields of sugarcane that
plunged its gnarled roots into a spiteful earth,
that entrapping us *just* outside of the rapture.

i ran off and found myself weighted down with my
birthright:
        being black and lynched
        being womxn and bruised
        being here and not here at all
being unable to leave the weakness in the trees;

so unlike the womxn who conjured us out of the rapes.

i couldn't run if i'd known how,

my momma never taught me.
or she did and i forgot
or she did and i didn't believe her

so, i laid prone and heavy, seeping into the earth.

she erased shame and resentment from my fingertips
and bathed my bare feet in a future rooted beyond
dirt and sharecropping, or bleeding and chain gang.

she turned me around in search for an unmapped place
and heard delusions that felt like spells tell me the truth:
we are the place. we will be the place. we were the place.

and when i rose, still in the fields, wet with secrets
i kissed the earth and cleaned it for me, for us, for them.

dear momma,

dear momma,

in therapy i taught myself to sit and breathe
instead of sigh; instead of screaming and running;
instead of drowning and vibrating

and when i sat down
with my pelvic bone to linoleum,
i studied up the word "selfishness"
and i tried to make you out of synonyms;
but the word's origins pointed back at me

me;
when i yelled at you for not being him,
when i yelled at you for being him,
when i yelled at you because i needed to yell at you,
and i needed to yell because i needed to yell at him.

me;
when i took from you
more than body and time in wombs,
more than breastmilk and sleep,
more than savings and dreams;
when i took you over and over and over again
leaving you bitter and exploited

me;
when i failed you,
and did what you said not to do,
because you said not to do it,
and made you pick up the pieces with me,
pick up the pieces of me,
pick up the pieces for me,
because i was so unable and incapable
and because i knew always would.

some mommas

some mommas are kind and pretty
and smell like lilac or lavender
and kiss you on your head when you're sick
and blow up raspberries on your tummy
and show you how to tie a ponytail
and teach you how to hide a receipt from daddy

and then they also drink
and forget their meds
and go manic and mean and red
and yell and hit and hurt
and blame and hate and never love

and then they put on make up and show you
some mommas are kind and pretty
and smell like lilac or lavender
and kiss you on the bruise they left on tuesday

my grandmother died an islander

my grandmother died an islander who unspooled
an anchor into a country that was disorienting and crude.

some mornings she beaded her knuckles into
white folk's clean laundry, and tended to their dirty kids
until her shirt back was sopping with violent sweat.

with rosaries inside of her hands, her and her husband
mangled together stale breadcrumbs and cornbread and
turned it into hallways peppered with laughter, high on jelly
and jam, babies ignorant of how quietly a spine can crack.

they weren't raised to know the stink of old dishwater
when it smashed hot onto your only good work clothes.

or how to disassemble a kitchen table before the landlord
comes back for the back rent spent on baby shoes.

or how shameful it feels to want for all that you need.

and yet, these babies grew uppity and unafraid
to let white teeth knotting against their shins and ankles.

clambering, they took everything from her house.
they bolted the escape door, leaving my grandmother's
dreams burning alive inside; gulping and gulping.

nothing made it out alive except me and the rosaries.

now i gotta kneed my knuckles into white folk's clean laundry
and tend to their dirty kids until my shirt back is
sopping with my violent sweat and my resentful tears and
my dream that my daughter's fingernails will never have
to scratch out the scent mildew left in her school clothes.

a baby is crying

a baby is crying
a baby is crying
    so loud

a baby is crying
    and it is so loud

a baby is crying
    and it is so red and loud
    it is so red and loud and painful

a baby is crying
    and it is so red and loud and painful
    and it wont stop it wont stop it wont

a baby is crying
    getting all red and loud and painful
    not stopping not stopping not stopping

a baby is crying
    dying the room in violent cherry red
    dousing the walls in violent red like cherries

a baby is crying
    and i cannot soothe them
    and i will not soothe them
    and i don't want to soothe them
        her red loud painful non stop
        make it stop make it stop make it stop

i am crying loud and red
and i don't know how to stop

ma,

ma,
i didn't want to mother you
                        this trauma

                    or myself
i just wanted to be sevenandahalf

iv. what do you know about cleaning up blood?

1. try

1. try to have heavy bleach at your side
weave it into the fabric immediately after the blood
      like *immediately* after the blood
      like spill bleach and the blood in chorus
other than that the blood will never lift off the couch

2. have that corporate-level sprinkle shit
(the one that eats away at the blood)
      think about it, have you ever seen blood at walmart
      even when you know there should be blood at walmart?

3. it's never as big of a deal as it looks
i say it's like heartbreak that way.

and another gospel as told by womxn

and another gospel as told by womxn:

my cousin died in his sleep
        they said "congestive heart failure"
        a chronic and progressive sickness
        one day pump pump pump
        the next day it gave up on itself

                                        gave up on him.

he sat there   dead   for two days.

                it's a long time to sit there   dead
                any time is a long time to sit there   dead

                                              i know that
                                        and i know this

                            bleach isn't enough to clean up
                                  the scent of blood
                                  the scent of death
                                the scent of a body
                                that done gave up

1. remember

1. remember, you can scrub
   scrub
   scrub
      until your fingernails splinter and prune
      but it will never be gone

2. remember, it will never be gone
      one day,
      you will sit
      wine in hand,
      puzzle book on lap

      and when you drop the pen cap
      (because we always drop the pen cap)
      you will see it:
            a spot that you lost track of
            a spot that you feel inside you.

3. remember, you can ignore it, but it won't be ignored.

blood on cotton panty fabric

blood on cotton panty fabric
turns ecru
smells like hot acid

blood on tampons
that were left like struggling levees
can be red and layered
like velvet cake
like a bloomed rose

blood on mattresses
seep down and lighten
but only in the middle;
on the edges it stays
hard and rich in pigment.
easily covered, though.

blood on penis
either turns him on
or it turns him off
but usually neither

blood on fingers
checking and verifying
made clean by toilet paper
fastened into quick diapers
folded into a womxns prayer
heavy with shame and heat.

soap and water and soap and water
and fingernails into palms
and fingernails into nailbeds
soap and water and soap and water
but you see the specks
pink and sweet stinking

like pussy

v. how can we love you better? and you, us?

love me better

love me better
hear me more
be accepting
unconditional
        unapologetic
considerate.

be the foundation
fortified like prayer
        breathe fresh
be eternal
make me internal

be patient
        be air and earth
and imperfect
and love and abled to
be love and love better.

ways to heal (#1)

enclose yourself in tenderness that manifests as
(kin)folk who know your middle name
and always make your coffee with cheap whiskey.

they'll love on you so much, you will become magic.

i need you

i need you to be present and out of reach and somewhere.

      send me an envelope and tell me where to be
so i can help you fold wrinkles and press napkins.
and if i can't, just know i would and let that hold weight.

sometimes the thought of your company fills space.

i need you patient and decent and sometimes kind.

      god made flaws and secrets so we could raise our own
unknowable tongue of jokes inside of jokes inside of us.
bury those secrets, and bring them out in intervals and
hold them to the red moon so you remember how to see me
when i have said the wrong thing and forgot and forgot.
and i will unmask your flaws and translate them into learning.

i need you to be vulnerable, happy, and bare.

      we spent a summer barking at the moon til we were pink
and filled ourselves with goat curry and old gossip.
but we couldn't stay in that heat; grounded and sustained
we had to stretch and grow the darkness into space.

      that past litters my time now with golden laughter and
when i feel it, callus like my bodiless hands, tired and old;
i call you because i miss you and you answer the same.
and we talk, conversations ongoing like endless cobwebs;
and that has to be good enough. we need it to be good enough.

and i need you to know that i need you, and us, and me.

look at me

look at me

again
look at me again

let me see myself

offer me myself
exhibit you yourself

you are myself
i am yourself
show me

look at me

i will look back
with our blueness
with our redness
all the teary colors

erase and paint us
a reflection
abstract and strange

this is the point of living
loving you
loving me
loving us

sis, come sit with me

sis, come sit with me
and let me love on you like
you love up on me.

mattafact tell me, sis
how you need to be loved?
need me to hold you?

bring you into me
to put your head down a sec
and let your skin exhale?

or can i sing you
a hymn my momma said makes
god lighten the soul?

quilt together quotes
to remind you aint no one
that's betta than you?

sis, i will stop time
to sit and burn every tear
and drown every sigh.

let me love on you
like how you loved on me
when ain't no one could

jamilla danae vandyke-bailey is the daughter of karyn vandyke and dana bailey, and stepdaughter to lita bailey. she is the granddaughter of kathryne vandyke and brenda chaney. she is the mother of dana-morrison sellassie awuye. she is a sister, aunt, cousin, friend, ex-girlfriend, and enemy. she is black. she is a poet. she is a writer. she is an educator. and she is womxn.

www.ingramcontent.com/pod-product-compliance
Lightning Source LLC
Chambersburg PA
CBHW020343170426
43200CB00006B/487